First published 1997
Reprinted 1999

ISBN 0 7110 2552 5

Published by Ian Allan Publishing

an imprint of Ian Allan Publishing Ltd,
Terminal House, Shepperton, Surrey
TW17 8AS.
Printed by Ian Allan Printing Ltd,
Riverdene Business Park, Hersham,
Surrey KT12 4RG.

Code: 9908/2

Front cover: 'Cathedrals Express'
passing through Sonning cutting
headed by No 7002 *Devizes Castle*.

Back cover: 'Modified Hall' class
No 7905 *Fowey Hall* pilots *King
George V* up Hatton bank with the
down 'Cambrian Coast Express'.

Right: 'Castle' No 5076 *Gladiator*
with the Hastings to
Wolverhampton express seen
between Hatton North and
Lapworth.

Picture credit
All photographs by the author.

GWR 4-6-0s IN COLOUR

COLLETT & HAWKSWORTH LOCOMOTIVES IN THE 1960s

Derek Penney

IAN ALLAN
Publishing

Introduction

A remarkable fact is that when the first withdrawal from service of a 'Castle' class engine took place in 1950, so durable was its design that there were in production at Swindon 10 new engines of near-identical construction to add to the 160 still in service. Moreover, when you consider that the design was essentially as laid down in the 'Star' class of 1907, it becomes clear how far ahead of its rivals the Great Western Railway was in the field of locomotive design in the early 1900s. It was a lead that was to be maintained for many years to come.

The man responsible for this happy state of affairs for the company was G. J. Churchward. He had set himself the twofold objectives of improving manufacturing standards, and of producing a range of standard locomotives, using as many common parts as possible. His method was to evaluate thoroughly, by practical trials on the road, all the possible options before formulating his final designs, and he was not shy of incorporating some features of locomotive design from abroad. Thus, two-cylinder 4-4-2 and 4-6-0 engines were matched against each other, against four-cylinder compound 4-4-2s from France, and they in turn against four-cylinder simple 4-4-2 and 4-6-0s. This approach was to pay handsome dividends, for the outcome was the adoption of two outstanding 4-6-0 designs: the two-cylinder 'Saints' and the four-cylinder 'Stars' mentioned above. A four-cylinder Pacific was also tried, but found inappropriate for GWR use, so the 4-6-0 tradition that the GWR was steadfastly to maintain became firmly established.

Though none of Churchward's locomotives appear in this book, all that do stem from those two key designs. C. B. Collett continued where his predecessor left off, quickly bringing out two notable 4-6-0 designs — the 'Castles', already remarked upon, and the rebuilding of Churchward's two-cylinder *Saint Martin* with smaller driving wheels as a prototype of the 'Hall' class, forerunner of many similar mixed-traffic 4-6-0 types on the GWR and elsewhere. When greater power was called for, he took the 4-6-0 type to its ultimate size with his four-cylinder 'King' class of 1927, and there later followed the more specialised 'Granges' and lightweight 'Manors'. Continuity was maintained under F. W. Hawksworth with the introduction of the 'Modified Hall' and the large, two-cylinder 'County' classes, until at last change seemed to be in the wind with the possibility of a new GWR Pacific. However, if this was anything other than rumour, it was quickly overtaken by the unified British Railways locomotive policy. So the 'Counties' completed the range of GWR 4-6-0s, but they were not the end of the story, as the performance of many of the 4-6-0s was to be enhanced still further under BR ownership by improvements to the draughting, and the adoption of higher superheat.

More than a brief outline of their origins would be inappropriate in a book of this nature, the more so since there are many scholarly accounts of these locomotives available to the public. Besides, whatever their merits as machines, it was their appearance that I — and, I suspect, many others — found the most fascinating of their attributes, and which is the focus of this book. The uniquely ornate styling — 'old-fashioned' but grandly so — was what first attracted me to them as a small boy. To *pictures* of them, I should say, because they were 'foreign engines' to me and I never actually set eyes on one until I was into my teens. True, I had caught sight of one or two newly-built '9400' class panniers leaving the Yorkshire Engine Co's works, but these were nothing compared to the thrill of sighting my first GWR 4-6-0, even though it was only a fleeting glimpse. It must have been at Ashendon Junction, as I journeyed on a school outing to London down the old Great Central line, that a 'Hall' in BR lined black livery with red-backed name- and numberplates, with all its brass and copper well burnished, stood awaiting our passing. Its appearance would have put our dirty 'B1' to shame, yet it was at the head of a *goods* train! Later that year, after much wheedling for parental permission — bear in mind it was the early 1950s — I spent my first full day of looking at Great Western engines at Birmingham

Snow Hill station, and can remember my amazement at how the 'Kings', blue at that time, made such clean and vigorous starts without any trace of wheelslip. I was not used to that from… well, never mind what!

Years later, when I began photographing trains in colour, the lure of the nearby East Coast main line and engines known from infancy was paramount, although the Western 4-6-0s were at the top of my 'some day, I must…' list. When the 'A3s' got their 'elephant ears' the day had clearly arrived, and I began in earnest to gather the pictures that follow. Of course, it was a race against time (in the guise of the BR dieselisation programme) and in defiance of the English climate with, as I recall, not much help from the Meteorological Office! With very few exceptions, the scenes depicted come from the years 1961 to 1963. It was a time when the GWR 4-6-0s, although on their way out, retained a good share of the main line express work, and still possessed much of the old Great Western charisma — or so I like to think. I hope this collection will give some pleasure as a portrait of that brief, but poignant, phase of their existence. Unfortunately, it also reflects a harsh world for steam locomotives, in which the new diesel motive power units increasingly claimed the lion's share of care and attention; yet I have not found it difficult to leave out pictures from the very last days of steam when engines ran nameless, numberless and utterly filthy. With regard to the factual content of this book, I have endeavoured to verify its accuracy where possible but so much is dependent on memory that, if errors of fact have intruded, I pray the reader will forgive me and allow that this book was conceived more for its appeal to nostalgia than as a work of historical reference.

I began with a tribute to the 'Castles' and make no apology now for having allowed them to dominate my selection, for these most aristocratic of engines were my favourites among the whole exalted family of GWR 4-6-0s. Such is my admiration, I can *almost* forgive them for beating an even more handsome engine back in 1925!

Bibliography

Of the many publications consulted, the following have provided particular help (and distraction!) during the preparation of this book:

Brian Haresnape, *Collett and Hawksworth Locomotives*, Ian Allan Ltd
RCTS, *Locomotives of the Great Western Railway*, Railway Correspondence and Travel Society
Michael Rutherford, *Great Western 4-6-0s at Work*, Ian Allan Ltd
Martin Smith, *Great Western Express Passenger Locomotives*, Argus Books

Magazines: *The Railway Observer*, *Steam World*

Acknowledgements

I offer sincere thanks to Derek Huntriss for his encouragement in getting my photographs into print, and to the Librarian of the National Railway Museum for allowing me to see timetables of the relevant period.

Derek Penney
Sheffield
April 1997

Right: The Great Western lives on in 1961 as No 5097 *Sarum Castle*, at the head of the rake of chocolate and cream coaches forming the 'Capitals United Express', approaches Tilehurst.

Left: These two photographs date from rather earlier than most in this book and are among the very few colour shots of steam trains that I took on the Bristol main line west of Swindon, for these services were among the first to be dieselised. The exact day in May 1959 that this picture was taken is unknown, but the train is the 11.15am from Paddington to Weston-super-Mare. The absence of the 'Merchant Venturer' headboard may mean this is the untitled Sunday train, though the coaches did have the name on the roofboards. The chocolate and cream livery which had been re-established for Western Region expresses, together with the green-liveried No 6024 *King Edward I*, made the spectacle as authentically 'Great Western' as I was likely to see. I remember the train was running so very late — it *must* have been Sunday! — that I had almost given up on it. When it finally swept round the curve, with that rapid, even

drumming of exhaust that only a 'King' could produce, its speed was such that I had scarcely time to scramble to my feet and sight-up.

Above: This was such a superb location — near Corsham, Wiltshire — that I wish I had visited it more often. An overbridge spanning the cutting now separates me from the spot where I had photographed *King Edward I*, as 'Castle' No 5090 *Neath Abbey* approaches from the opposite direction with an up express. This was one of the 'Castles' rebuilt from earlier 'Star' class engines in 1939. The frames of the 'Stars', in this case already 16 years old, must have been very strong to withstand the additional weight of the 'Castle' boiler. *Neath Abbey* was finally withdrawn in 1962 with a combined final mileage of over two million.

Above: My first visit to Hatton on the Birmingham to Paddington line was in August 1961. The intention was to photograph trains climbing the bank from Warwick, but lack of acquaintance with the surroundings initially led me in the opposite direction, to the high overbridge at Hatton North. At mid-afternoon on a summer Saturday the line was fairly humming with activity, so it seemed best to get on with the business there and then — which I did, and quickly secured two 'King' shots. With steam to spare, No 6002 *King William IV* is heading the 11.40am from Birkenhead to Paddington through the lush Warwickshire countryside.

Right: The northward prospect was pleasing so I proceeded in that direction but, by the time I reached the site of the end of the train depicted above, there was another 'King' approaching on a down express. Though the incline levels-off through Hatton station, there is still a bit of a climb beyond Hatton North Junction which No 6020 *King Henry IV* is tackling with the 1.10pm from Paddington to Birkenhead. A little further on from here I took the shot of *Gladiator* shown on the title page.

Left: Eventually I arrived at Lapworth water troughs just as 'Hall' class No 4940, absolutely filthy, came by with a Saturday 'extra'. This was followed by the 2.10pm from Paddington to Birkenhead headed by Stafford Road's No 6017 *King Edward IV* which is picking up water from the trough. The engine will have replenished its tender on the move twice before on its journey from London — at Ruislip and Aynho troughs. Note the well-trodden path along the cutting side, perhaps worn by railwaymen trying to avoid repeated soakings as they walked the line.

Above: The view northwards from the same spot as in the previous photograph is depicted here. *Earl Cawdor* had just headed south with a tremendous splash, too fast for my camera, followed more sedately by this 'Modified Hall', No 6979 *Helperly Hall*, heading a parcels train which I believe had originated at Shrewsbury. Although the more heavily used main lines had by this time mostly been relaid with flat-bottomed rails, the old bull-head rails still survived at these installations (note them also at Goring troughs, on page 51).

Left: I lingered at this location another hour or so and was rewarded with the sight of ex-works 'King' No 6007 *King William III* gracing the next down express, which I guess was the 3.10pm Paddington to Wolverhampton. One incident I remember when looking at this photograph is that, at the very last moment, another photographer appeared at my elbow, exchanged a few pleasantries as we took the shot, and then disappeared through the bushes as quickly as he had emerged. He was obviously familiar with the line and its workings and was expecting this very engine at this very time. I've often wondered who that person was and thought, in vain, that one day the mystery would be solved by seeing this picture reproduced with some well-known name beneath it.

Below: It was time to head home. As I made my way to the station No 6005 *King George II* passed with an up express. At Lapworth station I recorded this scene with 'Castle' No 7004 *Eastnor Castle* passing through with a down express. This train was untraceable in the timetable, and the appearance of a Worcester-based 'Castle' on this line was also something I had not been expecting. The station itself is probably unchanged from GWR days apart from the British Railways oval, enamelled nameplates.

Above: It had been an odd sort of day, not at all as intended, but in retrospect my original *faux pas* was fortuitous. Not only was I never again to have such a fine afternoon on the Lapworth section, but also, unbeknown to me at the time, the sun would have been moving into its least favourable position for trains climbing Hatton bank. My final shot of that day, 26 August 1961, was taken at Lapworth station. The sun was almost down as No 6015 *King Richard III* came tearing through with the 2.40pm Birkenhead to Paddington. Though by this time all the 'Kings' had their double chimneys, No 6015 had been the first to be fitted, in September 1955, and in the subsequent period when its performance was under the spotlight, was timed at speeds well in excess of 100mph.

Right: While selecting photographs for this book I realised that, despite the fact that the majority of them were mixed-traffic engines, I hadn't recorded many GWR 4-6-0s on freight duties. There are probably several reasons for this, but maybe this picture itself holds one or two clues. 'Hall' class No 5970 *Hengrave Hall*, a Pontypool Road engine, is seen passing through Sonning cutting about mid-morning. Therefore she would have been travelling for most of her journey from South Wales through the night — which is when most of the freight was moved along the trunk routes. Also, those motive power depots which specialised in freight workings often hadn't the staff available to keep their engines clean, hence the rather dirty condition of No 5970. In my notebook I had written: 'Dirty, but nice exhaust — *must* conserve film for clean!' So, evidently short of both film and funds at the time, I very nearly didn't take this one!

Left: I suppose one of the most photographed sections of the former GWR was that through Sonning cutting, east of Reading. It was almost a place of pilgrimage for anyone recording ex-GWR steam in action, and I was fortunate in visiting it several times. The next four photographs result from a session on 9 September 1961, the last Saturday of the summer timetable. No 7036 *Taunton Castle*, the penultimate 'Castle' to be built, is heading west with a Saturdays-only Paddington to Paignton train. Though the West of England services were by then mostly diesel-powered, steam was still used on summer extras during 1961 and the following year.

Above: During the summer of 1961, however, the South Wales services were still mainly steam-hauled. 'Kings' displaced from the West of England trains, and based for the first time in Cardiff, were very much in the frame. Earlier in the morning Nos 6004 and 6003 had gone up on the 'Capitals United' and Fishguard boat train, and now No 6023 *King Edward II* passes with an express from Cardiff. Pleasingly, the locomotive was not adorned with the large and unsightly train reporting numbers carried on most Western Region expresses, which were intended to make train recognition easy. No doubt on this section they would have been all the more important because of the sheer volume of traffic that passed, the West of England, Bristol, South Wales, Cheltenham and Worcester routes all having merged.

Above: If there was anything worse than the reporting number boards it was the chalked on numbers like these on No 5062, and they must have been most confusing to those who relied on them when they were left unerased from previous workings, as often happened. *Earl of Shaftesbury* was one of those 'Castles' which had their castle names replaced by those of earls. This followed the naming of No 5063 as *Earl Baldwin* when the ex-Prime Minister and GWR dignitary received his title. Not surprisingly, a 'me too' chorus from his fellow peers ensued and, as this led to 20 'Earl' names then carried by '9000' class 4-4-0s — nice little engines, but of rather mongrel origin — being transferred to the splendid new 'Castles', who could blame them? Coming back to this train, I

struggle to identify it, but as No 5062 had been recently transferred to Neath following the closure of Landore shed, I guess it would be from Swansea.

Right: Another 'Castle' name which was temporarily lost was No 5075 *Devizes Castle* which, in 1941, was renamed *Wellington* after the wartime RAF aircraft. Newly transferred to Neath shed, she is seen heading the 11.55am from Paddington to Pembroke Dock. At this time of year photography in the innermost depths of the cutting was hampered by shadows cast across the track due to the relatively low sun. A successful visit in high summer was a mission never accomplished.

Left: I suppose one of the most photographed sections of the former GWR was that through Sonning cutting, east of Reading. It was almost a place of pilgrimage for anyone recording ex-GWR steam in action, and I was fortunate in visiting it several times. The next four photographs result from a session on 9 September 1961, the last Saturday of the summer timetable. No 7036 *Taunton Castle*, the penultimate 'Castle' to be built, is heading west with a Saturdays-only Paddington to Paignton train. Though the West of England services were by then mostly diesel-powered, steam was still used on summer extras during 1961 and the following year.

Above: During the summer of 1961, however, the South Wales services were still mainly steam-hauled. 'Kings' displaced from the West of England trains, and based for the first time in Cardiff, were very much in the frame. Earlier in the morning Nos 6004 and 6003 had gone up on the 'Capitals United' and Fishguard boat train, and now No 6023 *King Edward II* passes with an express from Cardiff. Pleasingly, the locomotive was not adorned with the large and unsightly train reporting numbers carried on most Western Region expresses, which were intended to make train recognition easy. No doubt on this section they would have been all the more important because of the sheer volume of traffic that passed, the West of England, Bristol, South Wales, Cheltenham and Worcester routes all having merged.

boards it was the
been most
...ed from
...e of those
...This followed
...er and GWR
...m his fellow
...000' class
...g transferred to
...to this train, I

struggle to identify it, but as No 5062 had been recently transferred to Neath following the closure of Landore shed, I guess it would be from Swansea.

Right: Another 'Castle' name which was temporarily lost was No 5075 *Devizes Castle* which, in 1941, was renamed *Wellington* after the wartime RAF aircraft. Newly transferred to Neath shed, she is seen heading the 11.55am from Paddington to Pembroke Dock. At this time of year photography in the innermost depths of the cutting was hampered by shadows cast across the track due to the relatively low sun. A successful visit in high summer was a mission never accomplished.

Above left: A few days earlier I had photographed No 6009 *King Charles II* travelling through the cutting on the up relief line. Again the train is unidentified but, whatever its duty, No 6009 made a fine sight. These pictures perhaps give rather a false impression of what a morning in the cutting was like at the time because all the diesels, which would have amounted to about 50% of the workings, have been filtered out. That is to say, they were just not photographed! I understand that 'Warships', 'Hymeks' and the like have their enthusiasts today, and to them I apologise for remarking that these locomotives were, at the time, anathema to me.

Left: The best part of the day in Sonning cutting was the 2hr period each side of midday. After that the westering sun was not advantageous to photography

there; however, a good place to make use of this was Tilehurst station on the other side of Reading. There was a good, open layout to the east of the station and that is where I caught No 6004 *King George III* returning home to Cardiff with the 2.55pm Paddington to Swansea on 9 September 1961. The 'Kings' did not reign for long on these South Wales services which, a year later, were almost all being hauled by diesel traction.

Above: A few minutes later No 6024 *King Edward I* was passing through Tilehurst station in the opposite direction with the 1.40pm Saturdays-only from Weston-super-Mare, showing that 'Kings' were still performing occasionally on the Bristol road. Both this and No 6004 were withdrawn in June 1962, although No 6009 lasted until September.

found rather
ng south from
I managed a
his day, however,
eling
astle' No 5043
westbound —
Arms and
's cab is
been to get a
someone at some
sleepers on

Right: The view in the other direction at this delightful location is just as
enticing. On 19 August 1961, I secured this shot of 'Castle' No 5059
Earl St Aldwyn, which was by far the best sight all day, the weather having been
its usual indifferent self until late on, and the engines that passed, depressingly
dirty. This train is the Penzance to Liverpool express, and the Shrewsbury
locomotive heading it will be nearing the end of a long day, having worked
through from Devon. A few years later, this view of the line would become an
impossibility due to shrubbery having been allowed to flourish, as happened so
often when steam working ceased.

a visit to
...king in the spring
... *Athelhampton*
...d-of-all-work',
... work than any
... and cleanliness

Right: Here are two 'Castles', still separated from their tenders, which have just had the Swindon beauty treatment. No 5043 *Earl of Mount Edgcumbe* is one of those members of the class which came to be fitted with double chimneys and four-row superheater boilers, whereas No 7026 *Tenby Castle* still has the three-row superheater boiler she was built with in 1949. A total of 66 engines were 'modernised' in this way, but no more were dealt with after the end of 1961.

Left: Before visiting the works, I had photographed No 5064 *Bishop's Castle* standing near the station. A Swindon engine, and carrying the express-passenger headlamp code, she was probably waiting to take over an incoming service, or maybe is a standby pilot in case of failure. This engine has acquired one of the later Hawksworth tenders first introduced on the 'Modified Halls' and those 'Castles' built after the war. Though they looked well enough, the tenders just did not seem to suit these engines as much as the 4,000gal Collett tenders which the older engines had come to be fitted with, but they would undoubtedly have been simpler to construct.

Above: After visiting the works, there was the opportunity to photograph a few trains that departed before my own did. No 4080 *Powderham Castle* of Canton shed duly came and went, followed by No 4929 *Goytrey Hall*, heading into the sun from the same platform. The shedplate shows this to be a Gloucester engine and doubtless she was homeward-bound.

Left: On 31 March 1962, Fulham was pitted against Burnley in an FA Cup semi-final played at Villa Park, and five special trains were provided for the Fulham supporters, running at around 10min intervals ahead of the 'Cambrian Coast Express'. Nearing the top of Hatton bank is the first of these, hauled by 'Castle' No 7018 *Drysllwyn Castle*, to be followed by *Shrewsbury Castle*, *Sir Felix Pole* and *Barry Castle*. No 7018 is notable in having been the first 'Castle' to be fitted with a double chimney, back in 1958.

Below: By now the 'Cambrian' was due, and the sonic sensations that only a 'King' could produce seemed to herald its approach. But no, although a 'King' — No 6016 *King Edward V* —was certainly appearing round the curve, it was at the head of another special, this one apparently carrying the dignitaries and VIPs. I hope they were as satisfied with their team's 1-1 draw as the lineside photographers were with the splendid bonus on the day's haul of pictures! Six weeks earlier there had been an even more impressive cavalcade up the bank as eight 'Kings' and three 'Castles' conveyed Tottenham Hotspur supporters to West Bromwich. Alas, it probably goes without saying, on that occasion the weather was foul.

Right: The formidable banks between Newton Abbot and Plymouth, with gradients as steep as 1 in 40/1 in 50, posed the biggest challenge to the hill-climbing abilities of GWR passenger locomotives, and the 'Kings' were conceived to master them. In comparison, the four miles or so between Warwick and Hatton, with the gradient fluctuating between 1 in 95 and 1 in 110, was something these most powerful engines could take in their stride. I never saw a 'King' in difficulties on this section, certainly not No 6027 *King Richard I* which is approaching the top of the bank in fine style at the head of the 1.10pm from Paddington. A tendency for steam to leak from the inside cylinders of these engines, and the 'Castles', shows up in this picture. Quite a mild example of it, actually!

this rather dusty 'Modified Hall', No 6998 *Burton Agnes Hall*, was in charge, but I thought it worth including for the way the exhaust mimics the cumulus clouds in the distance. At the time, knowing that the days of steam were numbered, I would have been incredulous had someone predicted that I would again photograph this engine near this very spot, but 15 years on. That, of course, would be while it was working a special train, following preservation in private ownership.

Left: The 'Cornishman' was a cross-country express originating at Wolverhampton which, south of Birmingham, made its way via the Hatton North curve and the line through Stratford-upon-Avon and Cheltenham. As usual, on this spring day in 1962 it was powered from Wolverhampton by a Stafford Road 'Castle'. No 5031 *Totnes Castle*, which is seen approaching Lapworth, had been allocated to Stafford Road when new in 1934 and was withdrawn from there in October 1963. This 'Cornishman' train was soon to originate in Sheffield and be rerouted onto the Midland line through Birmingham.

Below: This late afternoon express from Birmingham to Paddington is approaching Lapworth on 14 April 1962 behind No 6017 *King Edward IV*. The first six 'Kings' to be withdrawn were to go in June that year and three others, including No 6017, followed them a month later.

... bank
... original
... and was
... made it the
... ny when
... 62, against

... ncy for
... be that,
... ains.

everyone moved up the pecking order leaving very few hands for cleaning. Even the 'Kings' suffered as can be seen in this shot of No 6014 *King Henry VII* wheeling the 7.40am Birkenhead to Paddington. 11am from Snow Hill, down Hatton bank. The engine is carrying a piece of its history around with it in the shape of the vee-fronted cab, a relic of the GWR's attempt to streamline this and No 5005 *Manorbier Castle* in the 1930s. The publicity conscious GWR evidently felt it must do something to counter the streamlined trains of the LMS and LNE Railways, but there is universal agreement that the results were awful and the streamlining was removed bit by bit, leaving only this feature on No 6014.

Left: A feature of summertime traffic on this line was the large number of through train workings between the Midlands and the South Coast. Most of these were Saturdays-only, but at least two operated all through the week and could be relied on to have photogenic motive power. One of these was the 10.42am (10.50am SO) Wolverhampton to Ramsgate, usually hauled by a well cleaned Reading-based 'Castle' which would have worked down with the corresponding train the day before. Here in the summer of 1962, I just managed to grab this shot of No 4096 *Highclere Castle* with its rake of Southern Region coaches before a rapidly approaching 'Western' diesel on the 'down' line cut off my view.

Above: Very creditably for this time of year, Oxford shed has managed to put a shine on No 7008 *Swansea Castle* before it took over the 9.20am Saturdays-only Bournemouth West to Wolverhampton, seen here ascending Hatton bank. Roughly parallel to the railway incline, the Grand Union Canal rises through a flight of 22 locks, sometimes called 'the 22 steps to heaven' by canal-folk. It was a very apt description in 1962 if you turned left at the top, to the bridge over the railway cutting!

...to watch the
... First to arrive
... closely
...arted Snow
... the
...ondon services
... 'Kings'
...ed until
... year.

Right: Another reason for the sudden demise of the 'Kings' was that, with their exceptional 22½ tons axle load and the restriction of route availability this imposed, they had simply run out of routes on which they could be used. In complete contrast, the next engine that passed had been designed with an axle load of no more than 17½ tons and could penetrate the remoter parts of the former GWR system from which all other 4-6-0s were prohibited. No 7817 *Garsington Manor*, from Stourbridge shed, one of a number of these engines allocated to the Wolverhampton district, is hauling the 10.20am Saturdays-only Birmingham to Margate. The signs of neglect on both these engines I have elsewhere suggested as being due to seasonal demands on men and machines, but another inescapable fact was that steam was on its way out and the focus of maintenance attention had shifted to the new motive power.

Left: A final picture on Hatton bank, before moving away from this favourite location, depicts No 4074 *Caldicot Castle*. This, only the second member of the '4073' class to be built, was the senior 'Castle' in service when this photograph was taken, No 4073 itself having already been withdrawn for preservation. Despite having been in service for some 36 years, *Caldicot Castle* was fully modernised in 1959 with double chimney and boiler with four-row superheater, as a result of which she would have been a more capable engine than many of the newer 'Castles'. The train is the 9.25am from Margate to Wolverhampton, which the locomotive will have worked from Reading.

Right: The Wolverhampton to Margate trains and the Reading 'Castles' that worked them provide the link with the next location. As the southbound train passes Tilehurst station it is nearly journey's end for No 4096 *Highclere Castle*, one of the earlier examples which retained the original style of inside valve casings at the front end. This engine attained one of the highest mileages recorded by a 'Castle' — 1,958,378 — when it was withdrawn exactly four months later.

Below: Approaching Tilehurst on the same day, 1 September 1962, with the reverse working from Margate to Wolverhampton, is No 5018 *St Mawes Castle*. On this day the train was about 30% heavier than when seen on Hatton bank in midsummer — a reflection maybe that many believed that late summer offered the best chance of good holiday weather. Notice that these trains used the relief lines between Didcot and Reading, where they passed to and from the Southern Region at Reading New Junction.

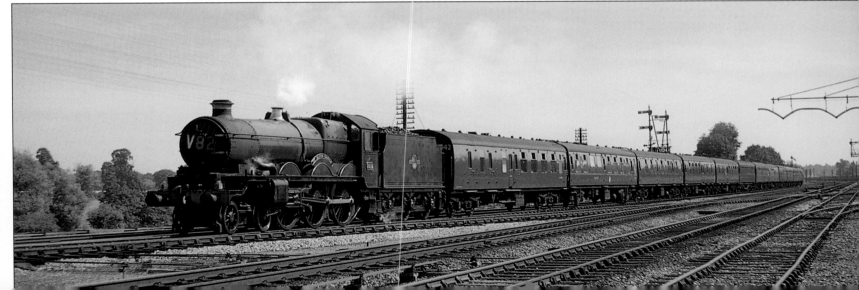

Right: As I turned to watch *Ince Castle* as she passed me, along came No 7031 *Cromwell's Castle* with the 1.15pm from Paddington to Worcester and Hereford, running a few minutes late. This was annoying as I had momentarily deserted my chosen viewpoint for this train in order to catch the Cheltenham. A wrong move, as it turned out, for No 7031 was the cleanest engine of the afternoon and this shot does not do her justice. I remember thinking as I released the shutter: 'What a waste of film!' But now I'm rather glad I did as it brings back memories of the day, with its little pains as well as pleasures. I don't know whether those passengers were amused or astonished at my antics, but I certainly hope they were not good at lip-reading!

...sant cutting
...empty
...the
...degenerated
...es ended

Right: A mile or two further on, at Tilehurst station, late afternoon sunshine steals through a heavily overcast sky to provide dramatic lighting for No 5097 *Sarum Castle* heading an up express. This Cardiff Canton engine, having lost the lustre of a year earlier (page 3) when she was working the 'Red Dragon' and return 'Capitals United' expresses, is probably deputising for a diesel.

Right: A few days later, 'Castle' No 5052 *Earl of Radnor* headed the heavily loaded train as it was photographed from the overbridge seen in the previous picture. Evidently Bristol's St Philip's Marsh shed had no cleaners at its disposal, as No 5052 had clearly been dirty for a long time. Withdrawal of this engine, as well as *Tintagel Castle*, plus 22 other 'Castles' and 12 'Kings', took place that month. Despite its dismal external condition, it is pleasing to note that *Earl of Radnor* was still fit for employment on Class '1' express duties right to the end.

Left: Small wonder that steam locomotives got so dirty, and so quickly, when you see the pall of smoke and soot being deposited from the chimney of No 4966 *Shakenhurst Hall* on all in its wake. The train is the 8.55am Saturdays-only from Sheffield to Bournemouth Central which will have been routed down the former Great Central line. I was expecting a much cleaner 'Hall', but it looks as if Banbury motive power depot had a problem and had to grab a visiting engine for the duty. No 4966 belonged to Oxley shed, Wolverhampton, miles off the route of this train, and would have been more accustomed to use on freight duties.

Above: The fireman takes a breather as No 4955 *Plaspower Hall*, looking altogether smarter than her sister engine and a credit to Taunton shed, comes along in the opposite direction. The original engine of this class, No 4900 *Saint Martin*, was a straightforward rebuild of the Churchward 'Saint' class 4-6-0 No 2925, with driving wheels reduced in diameter from 6ft 8½in to 6ft 0in. This rebuilt engine appeared in 1924, but it was not until 1928 that Collett began construction of the standard 'Hall' class with an initial order for no less than 80 locomotives, as part of which these two were turned out in 1929.

Left: Production of the 'Halls' continued steadily with only minor differences, right up to 1943. Substantial changes were introduced by F. W. Hawksworth, starting with No 6959 in 1944. These modifications were more concerned with methods of construction than the fundamental design, although a higher degree of superheating was incorporated. These '6959' class 'Modified Halls' were of strikingly different appearance, particularly when viewed from the front quarter. Their plate frame bogies and longer, steeply-angled steam pipes made them easy to recognise as they approached. Later, improvements to the draughting arrangement led to the use of a more slender chimney, without capuchon. Photographed from the same viewpoint as No 4955, this equally well cared for

'Modified Hall', No 7905 *Fowey Hall*, is at the head of the 11.4am Saturdays-only from Bournemouth Central to Sheffield Victoria on 8 September 1962.

Below: Earlier that week a session at Goring water troughs, although not notable for good fortune in terms of the synchronisation of sunshine with the steam trains that passed, did produce this shot of No 4948 *Northwick Hall* heading towards Reading with a very mixed goods train. Although travelling at only moderate speed, the locomotive is lifting water successfully enough to overflow the tender's top filler. Sadly, it would have been one of this 'Hall's' last outings as it was among the 75 GWR 4-6-0s to be withdrawn that month.

Left: The 1.15pm from Paddington to Worcester and Hereford was booked to be hauled by the engine which had brought that morning's 'Cathedrals Express' up to Paddington, and that usually meant a well polished 'Castle', like No 7031 *Cromwell's Castle* pictured here. The 'fireman's side' of a 'Castle' was definitely the best for viewing these superb engines, unencumbered by smokebox 'blisters', pipework, lubricators and the like, which cluttered up the other side a little. While the other railway Regions preferred the driving position on the left-hand side of the locomotive, the Western had it on the right and saw no more reason to change this than their lower-quadrant signals. The world would have stopped turning if it had!

Above: Despite the fact that increasing numbers of 'Hymek' diesels were at this time having a huge impact on steam operations, the Worcester line trains were to continue to be steam-hauled for a further year. The 10.5am from Hereford was usually powered by a Worcester 'Castle', but on this day it comes through the cutting at Purley behind Old Oak Common's No 5041 *Tiverton Castle*. This is one of the earlier 'Castles' which had in later life received a boiler with a three-row superheater, and one of the many which had their mechanical lubricators moved to the front of the platform, ahead of the steam pipe, and not to the benefit of the locomotives' appearance.

Right: Looking in the opposite direction, we see No 7023 *Penrice Castle* purring along with the 1.15pm down. She would have come up on the 'Cathedrals' and again, although turn-out is by no means a disgrace, things aren't what they used to be. My strongest memories of this day are of 2-8-0 No 4704 on an enormously long freight (which I can find no excuse to show in this book), and the bitterness of the cold weather. Fortunately a few yards up the road there was a pub with a roaring fire (and other comforts) which was visited more than once!

dieselised from
being taken
11.10am
However, an
-steam-
was not fully
until

Right: Also simmering gently at Worcester shed that day was No 7011 *Banbury Castle.* Although the shedplate clearly shows her to be a Reading engine, she is paying a visit to a former home, as I distinctly remember her being Worcester-based in the immediately preceding years. A number of 'Castles' were to remain at Worcester (and Hereford) in the following year to cover the diesel shortage and to act as standbys. This engine was also to survive until February 1965, being withdrawn then from Oxley shed, along with No 7023.

Worcester
Evesham, it
1.10pm
for a speed

Right: Passing through the station in the opposite direction, No 7004 *Eastnor Castle* had charge of the 11.15am out of Paddington, the engine returning home after working the 7.35am up from Worcester. Note that the tiny station has only a siding and a headshunt for handling its goods traffic, with not even a loading platform, let alone a goods shed. Nevertheless, in those pre-motorway days, business appears to be good, with the siding well occupied.

Left: On a later and very blustery day in the early spring of 1963, No 7002 *Devizes Castle*, on an up express from Worcester, is recovering from the speed restriction over the Avon bridge. This slowing was quite a handicap because there was little chance to recover speed before the obligatory Evesham stop. In fact, the 2½hr or so timing between Worcester and London was well below that of prewar days, though there were now more stops and the trains ran at even intervals both ways.

Above: Two hours later I was photographing the next London-bound train, hauled by 'Castle' No 7005 *Sir Edward Elgar*. The view is from the overbridge at the north end of Evesham station, with the former Midland line to Ashchurch and Tewkesbury going off to the left in the middle distance. The locomotive, allocated to Worcester shed throughout its 18yr life, was originally named *Lamphey Castle*. It was renamed around the time that the 'Cathedrals Express' was inaugurated in 1957 and was a frequent performer on it. Elgar was a native of Worcestershire, and was closely associated with the 'Three Choirs' music festivals, held in the cathedrals of Worcester, Hereford and Gloucester. Whether that was the intended connection, it was one that I always made.

... 1962 near
... ference a year
... ned 'Castle' at
... safety valve
... climb into the

Right: The line rises on a gradient of 1 in 100 for over four miles between Honeybourne and Chipping Campden. This was usually a very severe check for up trains but, with ample power in the shape of 'Modified Hall' No 7900 *St Peter's Hall* and an unidentified 'Castle', this train is topping the bank with the ease you might expect if it was bowling along the Thames Valley.

rking
 the
 rel.
 It is
 of the
 tern
 to
 n

Right: Shortly afterwards, this lightweight stopping train with its mixture of non-corridor coaches and a few vans also had the benefit of super-power at the front end. This was the easiest of tasks for Oxford's smartly turned out 'Hall', No 6927 *Lilford Hall*, strolling away from Chipping Campden on 23 June 1962. The practice of conveying goods vans by passenger trains diminished as this kind of service became the preserve of diesel multiple-units, some of which lacked the necessary reserve of power.

Left: No 7013 *Bristol Castle* was one of the oldest 'Castles' despite being numbered in the postwar '7000' series. Originally No 4082 *Windsor Castle*, it exchanged identities with No 7013 when its condition at the time made it unsuitable for hauling the funeral train of King George VI to Windsor in 1952. In spite of her age the engine has been fully modernised with four-row superheater and double chimney, and was uniquely fitted with a Davies and Metcalfe Patent valveless lubricator, the unsightly reservoir of which is all too visible on the side of the smokebox. The train is the 7.35am from Worcester, photographed near Ascott-under-Wychwood where, as can be guessed from the soot deposits on the overbridge, the line is now on a falling gradient.

Above: For a final picture of 4-6-0s on the Worcester line, what better than an immaculate 'Castle' on the 'Cathedrals Express', the most abiding image of the line from the short time that I knew it. No 7007 *Great Western* is taking advantage of the easy gradients beyond Ascott-under-Wychwood as the line follows the Evenlode down to Oxford. Built in 1946 and named *Ogmore Castle*, No 7007 was renamed in 1948 to commemorate the railway company that had just ceased to exist, it being the last 'Castle' to be built by the GWR. The name *Ogmore Castle* has at one time or another been carried by four 'Castle' class locomotives: No 5056, later *Earl of Powis*; No 5080, later *Defiant*; No 7007 and finally coming to rest on No 7035.

have
...es named

...t were
...t2 that as
...ed maybe it
...rtin. As it
...6ft 0in
...to be built.
...on
...e at
...the
...himneys

Right: This view of No 6853 *Morehampton Grange* under the wires at Crewe, in or around October 1964, shows the locomotive in splendid condition for the period. With a good fire and head of steam, she seems eager for the 'right-away' — but to where? Alas I cannot say, as I have no record of this day and no memory, even, of why I was passing through Crewe, unless it was for a last look at 'Manors' on the Cambrian lines. The red spot on the cab side denotes the route availability of these engines and shows it to be more restricted than the 'blue-spot' 2-6-0s they replaced. The black 'D' and white 'X' are indications of the power and haulage capacity. This GWR-devised system continued to be used by the Western Region in spite of the existence of a BR scheme based on LMS practice.

Right: Due to their more restricted route availability, the 'Granges' could not be regarded as true replacements for the Churchward 'Moguls' in the way that the lighter 'Manor' class 4-6-0s could. The first 12 of these were built in 1938, with an intended use on secondary, cross-country routes, although several years passed before they began to be used on the former Cambrian lines, from which I best remember them. In September 1964, No 7819 _Hinton Manor_ is near Hanwood, six miles or so out from Shrewsbury, with a train for Aberystwyth. The nearer track, which has been lifted, was taken out of use when the line to Minsterley was closed.

working
yth
1963. At
Pwllheli
n the
ge
best

Right: The driver of No 7801 *Anthony Manor* poses proudly with his engine at Machynlleth shed in August 1963. The steaming of the 'Manors' left something to be desired until, in 1951-2, the authorities at Swindon conducted experiments on No 7818 which led to improvements in the draughting, including the fitting of more slender chimneys to the whole class. This, along with their smaller 3,500gal tenders, emphasised their lean, almost dainty appearance which, for me, made them the most winsome of engines.

... took this long-
... in August
... Manor and
... were also
... some repainting

... side platform
... Dovey a little

while later, these two delightful little engines making a fine sight as they skirt the Dovey estuary. Looking at this photograph I am struck by the thought — fanciful, maybe — that though these engines were built as late as 1950, when viewed at this distance and angle they could almost be Churchward engines from well-nigh half a century earlier. 'Oh, that's because the GWR was ultra-conservative in its locomotive policy' some will say, but I think it shows how far ahead of the field Churchward was in his time, and how secure were the foundations he left for his successors to build on.

Left: Introduced in 1945, the 'County' class was the final GWR 4-6-0 design and had a boiler similar in size to the LMS '8F' 2-8-0s, some of which had been built at Swindon in the war years. However, the working pressure was increased to 280lb/sq in, the highest of any GWR 4-6-0. The squat double-chimneys with which the class came to be fitted rather spoiled their appearance, looking almost comically small in relation to the safety valve bonnet, particularly when viewed from the side. No 1015 *County of Gloucester* was photographed at Swindon works in April 1962 following repairs which had included only a partial repaint. It looks as if someone has cleaned up the nameplate support, perhaps as a hint to

the staff at Didcot shed of how good the paintwork could look with just a little elbow grease.

Above: Unfortunately, I did not get many colour shots of these engines in sunny conditions, but for a picture of a 'County' on the road, here is No 1021 passing Tilehurst with the 11.35am from Weston-super-Mare on 1 September 1962. A curious thing about these engines was the surging motion that you felt — a bit like being on the cakewalk — when riding behind them in the leading coaches, especially when they were coasting.

timetable was something of a watershed for Western Region main line steam. So many engines were withdrawn, and of the main-line services, only those to Worcester and Hereford were to remain regularly steam-hauled. I wonder if any of those spotters at Reading General realised they would not get another day of steam-working there as good as the one that was just drawing to a close? No, they couldn't have, for I don't think I realised it myself at the time. Anyway, would they have cared? They would probably have shouted 'Scrap it!' at the 'Castle', as was their cruel custom, and got ready to cheer the next 'Hymek' through! It would be gratifying, though, if just one of them were to pick up this book and remember, with the pleasure that I do, God's Wonderful 4-6-0s.